THE LIBRARY OF FAMOUS WOMEN

MARIAN WRIGHT EDELMAN

Defender of Children's Rights

by
Steve Otfinoski

A BLACKBIRCH PRESS BOOK

WOODBRIDGE, CONNECTICUT

Published by Blackbirch Press, Inc.
One Bradley Road
Woodbridge, CT 06525

©1992 Blackbirch Press, Inc.
First Edition

Printed in Hong Kong

10 9 8 7 6 5 4 3 2

Library of Congress Cataloging-in-Publication Data

Otfinoski, Steven.
    Marian Wright Edelman: defender of children's rights/Steven
Otfinoski. — 1st ed.
      (The Library of famous women)
      "A Blackbirch Press book."
      Includes bibliographical references and index.
      Summary: A biography of the Afro-American lawyer and social
reformer who is known for her work on behalf of children's rights.
      ISBN 1-56711-029-0
      1. Edelman, Marian Wright—Juvenile literature. 2. Afro-Ameri-
cans—Biography—Juvenile literature. 3. Civil rights workers—United
States—Biography—Juvenile literature. 4. Social reformers—United
States—Biography—Juvenile literature. 5. Children's rights—United
States—History—20th century—Juvenile literature. [1. Edelman,
Marian Wright. 2. Afro-Americans—Biography. 3. Children's rights.]
I. Title. II. Series.
E185.97.E33085   1991
973'.049607302—dc20
[B]   91-598
                                                       CIP
                                                        AC

Contents

Introduction

The date was April 4, 1968—one of the darkest days in America's history. On that day, civil rights leader Martin Luther King, Jr., was assassinated as he stood on a balcony of the Lorraine Motel in Memphis, Tennessee. King represented the hopes and dreams of millions of black Americans yearning for equality. In one reckless moment, those dreams were shattered. Many blacks believed their cause was now a lost one. In despair, they turned to violence. Riots broke out in the black ghettos of many American cities.

In Washington, D.C., a 28-year-old black lawyer and social activist still believed there was hope for the future. The day after King's death she encountered a group of angry black teenagers who felt differently. The young woman tried to reason with them. She told the youths that if they gave

Marian in 1960, age 21.

(Opposite page) **Martin Luther King, Jr. (second from right) led a march for civil rights in Montgomery, Alabama in 1965. Also marching with him were his wife, Coretta Scott King (right), Dr. Ralph Bunche (far left), and Andrew Young (right foreground).**

in to the violence they felt in their hearts, they would ruin their future.

One of the black youths stared at the pretty, middle-class woman and said, "Lady, why should I listen to you? I ain't got no future."

Those words made a deep impression on the woman. She was struck by the fact that the young man, and thousands of black teenagers just like him, believed they really had no future. She would not forget his bitter words. And she would always remember the hopelessness behind them. The young woman's name was Marian Wright, and this chance meeting changed the direction of her life. It drove her to find some way to bring hope back into the lives of America's poor and forgotten young people.

Chapter 1

A Caring Childhood

Marian Wright was working to help other people long before that fateful day in Washington, D.C. She grew up caring and committed to social change. Marian was born on June 6, 1939, in the town of Bennettsville, South Carolina. The youngest of five children, she was named after the black singer Marian Anderson.

Marian, about 6 years old.

A Model Family

Marian's father, Arthur Wright, was a minister at the local Shiloh Baptist Church. He practiced what he preached, putting his Christian faith to work as a leader of the black community. Bennettsville, like most Southern towns in the 1940s, was segregated. That meant black people lived apart from white people. It also meant that blacks lived in poorer neighborhoods. They had the lowest paying jobs. And their

7

children went to inferior schools. These schools were far below the standards of the schools for white children. Classrooms were unheated, textbooks were falling apart, and students often had to share books because there weren't enough for everyone.

There was no playground for black schoolchildren in the town, so, Reverend Wright constructed a playground behind his church, complete with a merry-go-round. He also founded a home for blacks who were too poor to live on their own. It was named the Wright Home for the Aged.

Marian's mother, Maggie Leola Bowen Wright, was just as committed as her husband. But Maggie usually worked quietly in the background. She raised money for her husband's church.

The Wrights raised their children to be hard-working and socially conscious. "Working for the community was as much a part of our existence as eating and sleeping and church," recalls Marian. "I did it as a kid like other kids go to the movies. It is what I was raised to be."

The children were urged by their parents to do their best in whatever task they took up. Homework had to be done every

(Opposite page)
A family portrait in front of Reverend Wright's church features mother Maggie and father Arthur, with Marian in the left foreground. The young woman behind Mrs. Wright is a family friend.

The house in which Marian grew up still stands in Bennettsville, South Carolina.

night. "If you said the teacher hadn't assigned you anything, Daddy would say, 'Well, assign yourself,'" remembers Marian's brother Harry. "It was just read, read, read."

Marian was a good student with a likeable, outgoing personality. A pretty girl, she was a drum majorette in the school band. However normal and happy her life might have seemed to be, the ugliness of racial prejudice was never far away.

One of Marian's childhood friends stepped on a nail and became seriously ill from the infection. Because he was black and poor, he couldn't get proper medical attention and soon died.

A classmate broke his neck jumping into the town creek from a bridge. The accident might never have happened if black children had been allowed to swim in the "whites only" public swimming pool. "I later learned that the creek where blacks swam and fished was the hospital sewage outlet," Marian says.

Then, one night in 1954, death hit even closer to home. Arthur Wright suffered a serious heart attack. Fourteen-year-old Marian went off in the ambulance with her stricken father. She recalled the experience to newscaster Harry Reasoner in a "60 Minutes" interview: ". . . he, in that ambulance, made it very clear to me that I, as a black girl, could be anything, do anything, and how important it was not to let anything get between me and my education and everything I could be."

College and a Year Abroad

Arthur Wright died before the ambulance reached the hospital. The family carried on, the way he would have wanted them to. Marian's mother continued running the Wright Home for the Aged. Marian's brother, Harry, replaced his father as minister of Shiloh Baptist

"I was taught that the world had a lot of problems; that I could struggle and change them; that intellectual and material gifts brought the privilege and responsibility of sharing with others less fortunate; and that service is the rent each of us pays for living."

Marian stands with her mother after graduation at Spelman College in 1960.

Church. And Marian, in 1956, entered the freshman class of Spelman College in Atlanta, Georgia.

Spelman was not her first choice for a college (she wanted to join her sister at Fisk). Spelman was the oldest college for black women in the United States. And had a somewhat conservative reputation. Students were required to wear hats and gloves whenever they went off campus. Curfews were strictly enforced.

But Spelman also had an important civil rights connection. Martin Luther King's sister was a teacher there, and still is today. King himself visited the college regularly. All this would be important to Marian in the future.

In her junior year, Marian received a fellowship to live and study abroad. She spent a happy summer in Paris, France, and spent the fall in Geneva, Switzerland. Then a dream came true for the young girl. A Lyle fellowship enabled her to make a study tour of the Soviet Union.

"I'd been dying to go to Russia ever since reading Tolstoy," she has said, referring to the famous Russian novelist. She arrived in Moscow at an exciting time. Soviet Premier Nikita Khrushchev had opened up

a new dialogue with the Western nations, especially the United States.

Although Marian didn't agree with the communist system of the Soviet Union, she fell in love with the Russian people. She returned to Spelman for her senior year with renewed energy and optimism. "That year gave me a sense of confidence that I could navigate in the world and do just about anything," she now says.

Cars and buses travel the snowy streets of Moscow, Russia in 1958. Marian spent a few months in the Soviet Union before her senior year in college.

Taking a Stand

Marian came home to find that the struggle for civil rights had spread to black colleges. In February 1960, four students from a black state college in North Carolina started a sit-in demonstration at a segregated lunch counter. It was illegal at that time for blacks in the South to use the same public bathrooms, drinking fountains, or lunch counters as whites.

A month later, black students in Atlanta were ready to stage their own demonstration. Marian's parents had taught her that segregation was wrong. Now she was ready to take a personal stand against it.

One day she posted a notice in her dormitory that read, "Young ladies who can picket, please sign below." Many of them did. They joined students from other black colleges and sat in at Atlanta's City Hall cafeteria. Fourteen Spelman "ladies" were arrested for participating. Marian Wright was one of them.

"It never occurred to me not to get arrested," she said. "I called my mother beforehand and told her what I was going to do, and she didn't object, although I know she was worried."

Up until then, Marian was planning to go on to graduate school. She wanted to major in Russian Studies. She felt this would prepare her for a career in the foreign service. But now, she saw she could fulfill a more important need.

One day while at Spelman, she did some volunteer work at the local office of the National Association for the Advancement of Colored People (NAACP). Marian was amazed at the number of complaints the office received, and how many people who needed help could not afford it. "And I got so angry at the number of people— poor people, black people, because many white lawyers back then wouldn't take civil rights cases—who had come to the local office needing legal help and couldn't get it," she recalls.

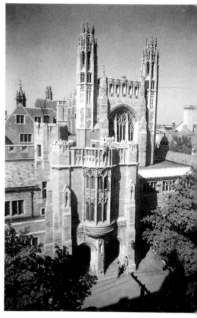

After receiving a fellowship in 1960, Marian enrolled at Yale Law School, in New Haven, Connecticut.

Marian decided to become a lawyer to help these people. She felt she had little aptitude for the law, but she remembered her father's advice. He had told her she could do anything she put her mind to and she believed it.

Marian applied for a fellowship to Yale Law School. She got the fellowship and entered Yale in the fall of 1960. It was the start of a new decade—a decade that would change the face of America and the life of Marian Wright.

Chapter 2

Lady Lawyer

It was hard for Marian to sit in her Yale law classes while others were working for civil rights full time. "But I made many good friends," she recalls.

Marian delivers an address at Stanford University in California.

Some of her friends were involved in a newly formed student civil rights group called the Student Nonviolent Coordinating Committee (SNCC). Although SNCC would become more radical by the mid-sixties, in 1960 its prime goal was to organize black and white students in peaceful demonstrations against segregation in the South.

Working in Mississippi

One of SNCC's target states was Mississippi. Mississippi has traditionally had a larger proportion of black people than any other state. It also had, and still has, many of the poorest black people in the nation.

(Opposite page)
In the 1960s, many college students demonstrated in an effort to gain equal rights for blacks. The "sit-down strike" was a common form of protest.

❖

"There is no free lunch. Don't feel entitled to anything you don't sweat and struggle for."

In the early sixties, the governing system in Mississippi was very racist. Segregationist and anti-black laws had the full support of the police, the courts, and the lawmakers.

SNCC workers set up offices in Mississippi and other Southern states to help blacks register to vote. By bringing blacks into the political process, SNCC hoped to give them a voice in government. They could then use their voting power to change unjust laws.

During spring break in her third year at law school, Marian went to Greenwood, Mississippi, to help in SNCC's office there. This time, she promised her mother she would not get arrested. On her arrival in Greenwood, Marian immediately aroused the curiosity of the local people. "The black people had all heard that a lady lawyer from up North was coming—me," she recalls. "They'd expected to see some well-dressed hotshot, and when I showed up in jeans I could see they were disappointed. After that, I always tried to look good."

On her last day, Marian was helping SNCC field secretary and friend Bob Moses register black residents at the local courthouse. The local white police didn't like these "outsiders" educating black people about their rights. The police attacked the SNCC workers with German shepherd police dogs. It was an experience Marian has never forgotten. "If I see a German shepherd on the street, to this day I'll cross over to avoid him," she says.

The police let Marian go, but a number of SNCC workers went to jail. They stayed there for several weeks, until the bail money arrived from SNCC headquarters. The experience strengthened Marian's resolve to become a lawyer and fight such abuses of the law.

Before the 1960s, many southern states were segregated. That meant blacks were forced to use facilities separate from the ones used by whites.

First Black Woman Lawyer

Marian returned to Yale and finished law school. She immediately signed on as one of the first interns in a program sponsored by the NAACP Legal Defense and Education Fund. For a year, Marian trained in New York City. She learned how to provide legal assistance for Southern blacks in civil rights cases.

When her year's training was completed, she was told she could work anywhere she chose in the South. She chose to return to Mississippi, where she felt she could do the most good. In the spring of 1964, Marian arrived in Jackson, the state capital. She was paid $7,200 a year to run a legal office.

Black teens marched in Selma, Alabama, in 1965 in an effort to gain equal rights to vote.

The Right to Vote: A Chronology

Marian was part of the fight to get black Americans registered to vote in the early 1960s. That fight was aided by ground-breaking civil rights legislation. Until the sixties, unfair poll taxes and literacy tests—aimed at the poor and undereducated—prevented many blacks from voting. Here are some of the laws that made black voter registration a reality.

1960—The Civil Rights Bill sets up the appointment of referees to help blacks register to vote.
1964—The 24th Amendment to the Constitution is adopted. It bars unfair poll taxes in federal elections.
1965—The Voting Rights Act makes literacy tests for potential voters illegal in most Southern states.
1966—A Supreme Court decision prohibits poll taxes in local and state elections.
1970—A new law makes literacy tests in all states illegal.

"That summer I very seldom got a client out of jail who had not been beaten by white police officers, who didn't have bones broken or teeth missing," she recalls. One boy she represented was shot and killed while in jail. Marian herself lived with the daily threat of violence and death.

"It's amazing what you can come to accept as part of your life," she has said. "Like starting up your car in the morning

Thousands mass together in front of the chapel in Selma, Alabama, to begin a 50-mile march to the capitol in Montgomery. The march, led by Martin Luther King in 1965, was to protest voting regulations.

with the door open in case there's a bomb. Bombs were going off all the time that summer, but you learn how to deal with that fear, and with the fear of being shot at; you learn how to function in spite of it."

As a legal counselor—before she became a lawyer—Marian learned the importance of "staying cool." White racists she knew wanted nothing better than to get her angry. By remaining professional and maintaining control, she was able to better help her clients and avoid trouble herself.

After living in Mississippi for a year, she took the bar exam. The bar is a test people need to pass to become lawyers. "I was the only black taking the exam," she remembers, "and they were astonishingly nice to me." Marian passed the bar exam and became the first black woman lawyer in Mississippi.

Enlisting in the War on Poverty

As she continued to work for civil rights, Marian came to an interesting conclusion: as a lawyer, she could only help one individual at a time to fight the system. She wanted to find a way to bring all black people together to confront the racism in their lives. Then they could fight from a position of real strength. To do this, Marian decided, the black community had to be organized.

Meanwhile, in the nation's capital, exciting things were happening. President Lyndon Johnson, who became president when John Kennedy was assassinated in November 1963, had recently been elected to a full four-year term. Johnson was a skillful politician and a firm believer in civil rights. He set out to pass Kennedy's series of major civil rights bills that would give black Americans political equality.

Johnson also launched a national "War on Poverty"—a massive federal program that would rebuild urban neighborhoods and create new jobs for the unemployed. One program to be included in this "war" was the Head Start project. This program provided federal funds to serve the needs of preschool children in poor families. Head Start centers were set up in local

Martin Luther King arrives at the Montgomery capitol after a five-day march from Selma.

President Lyndon Johnson worked hard to create and pass much civil rights legislation in the 1960s. He also dedicated himself to fighting poverty in America.

communities across the nation. These centers provided education, nutrition, meals, and social and medical services for local families.

The money for these programs was supposed to be given to each state—they had only to ask. Mississippi, where the need for Head Start was perhaps the greatest, refused to apply for the funds. Conservative state politicians didn't really want to help those who were poor and black.

Marian was angered by the state's lack of concern. She knew how much this money was needed in Mississippi. In April 1965, religious and civil rights groups, including the Delta Ministry of the National Council of Churches, formed an organization to get federal funds for the children of Mississippi.

Chapter 3

"People Are Starving"

Marian became the general counsel for the new agency, called the Child Development Group of Mississippi (CDGM). "It was one of the most exciting educational programs for poor folks in the nation," Marian says proudly, looking back.

Marian, in the early 1970s.

CDGM received 1.5 million dollars from Head Start in its first year and used the money to help 12,000 children. The organization's approach to helping families was a model of community participation. Members worked at the grass roots level, helping people to help themselves by getting directly involved in programs.

Marian Finds a Champion

But the conservative white political establishment in Jackson was skeptical. John Stennis, Mississippi's powerful senator, accused CDGM's main office of "racial agitation" and the misuse of federal funds. Rather than rely on federal funding that could be cut off, some members of the organization believed it would be better to drop this support entirely and rely on private contributions. Marian Wright disagreed. "I saw a lot of kids who were hungry," she recalls. I thought our first obligation was to the children and to the poor."

In April 1967, the U.S. Senate's Subcommittee on Employment, Manpower and Poverty held a public hearing on poverty in Jackson. One of the four senators who attended the hearing was Robert Kennedy, the younger brother of the late President John Kennedy. Robert had been attorney general in his brother's administration. In 1964, he had been elected senator from New York State. He was a passionate and caring politician who was in search of a cause. Marian Wright helped give him one.

Marian was one of the people who testified at the public hearing. Her testimony was a powerful plea for the poor people of Mississippi. "People are starving," she told the senators. "There is absolutely nothing for them to do. There is nowhere to go, and somebody must begin to respond to them. I wish the senators would have a

Senator Robert Kennedy was deeply moved by the pleas for aid Marian made in Washington. Kennedy soon became an important supporter of Marian's cause.

❖

"The 1990s struggle is for America's conscience and future. . . . The bombs poised to blow up the American dream [come] from no enemies without. They are ticking away within ourselves, our families, our communities and our lack of community, and our moral drift."

chance to go around and just look at the empty cupboards in the Delta and the number of people who are going around begging just to feed their children."

Kennedy and his colleague, Senator Joseph Clark of Pennsylvania, listened and took Marian up on her offer. Three days later, they went on a tour of the Delta Country with Marian as their guide. Everywhere they saw poverty and misery.

"We just went into individual houses of poor people, and knocked on their doors, sat down and talked to them, looked into their refrigerators, asked them what they had for breakfast, asked them what they had for supper," recalls Marian.

The most memorable moment for her came when they entered a shack in Cleveland, Mississippi, and stepped out of the range of the accompanying TV cameras. Robert Kennedy, Marian remembers, "saw a baby sitting over in a corner, a dark corner—with a bloated belly—and he got down with that baby and tried to get a response and couldn't. And he was visibly moved and angry, as he should have been. But that was, I think, the beginning of his real commitment to ending hunger in this country."

An Unlikely Romance

Returning to Washington, Kennedy urged the secretary of agriculture to send people from his department to Mississippi to see what he had seen and do something to help feed these hungry people. Senator Kennedy's bright, young legal assistant, Peter Edelman, was sent back to Mississippi to accompany the group from the Agriculture Department.

Edelman was from Minneapolis, Minnesota, and had gone to Harvard Law School. After clerking for the Supreme Court, he became a lawyer with the Justice Department. In 1964, he joined the staff of Robert Kennedy's campaign. He had been working for Kennedy ever since.

Peter Edelman had met Marian one night back in April just before the public hearing. He had been sent ahead of the subcommittee to discuss Marian's participation. She had work to do that night, but agreed to meet him for dinner. They talked about the issues that concerned them both. "We got together over hungry children," Marian explains, smiling.

When he called her on his next trip to Mississippi, Peter remembers, "It became clear that something was developing between us." What attracted this young black woman from the South to this white Jewish man from the Midwest? "We shared values," she says. "He's a kind man who I thought would also be big enough to let me be me. And that's not easy for somebody, I suspect."

In March 1968, Marian moved to Washington, D.C. It was a crucial decision. "How long could you live in a place like Mississippi, in that kind of life, without becoming a very different person?" she later said. Now she could continue her work for the poor where it would do the most good—in the capital. She would also be closer to Peter.

With a grant from the Field Foundation, Marian founded the Washington Research Project to report on the country's poor and underprivileged. Her goal was to be a voice for America's poor people and to see that laws to protect them were enforced.

It was to be a sad spring for America. Martin Luther King, Jr., was assassinated in April. Robert Kennedy, Marian's other hero, was shot to death at a Los Angeles hotel in June. Just moments before he was killed, Kennedy had won the California Democratic primary for the upcoming presidential race.

It was a time of despair for many Americans, certainly for Marian Wright and Peter Edelman. But on July 14, 1968, they were married in the backyard of a friend's house in Virginia. It was the first interracial marriage in the state since the Supreme Court struck down state laws that made such marriages illegal. The newlyweds went off on a five-month trip around the world that combined work and pleasure. Peter gave frequent speeches and Marian observed poverty firsthand in Africa, India, Indonesia, and Vietnam, where American troops were fighting a hopeless war against the North Vietnamese.

On July 14, 1968—in McLean, Virginia—Marian Wright married Peter Edelman at the home of a friend.

Failure and a New Beginning

When they got back to Washington, Peter became the associate director of the Robert F. Kennedy Memorial. Marian continued to work on her Washington Research Project. Moved by the despair of the black youth she had talked with after King's assassination, Marian decided to do a full report on education in America.

She got involved in the legislative process and helped draft a child development bill that would give more health and education aid to preschoolers. If children, especially poor children, could be helped at an early

Hunger and severe poverty were widespread throughout the South in the 1960s.

age, she thought, they had a better chance of being successful in life.

The child care bill was vetoed after passing both houses of Congress by then President Richard Nixon. Nixon, taking the line of many conservatives, claimed the bill would weaken the family. Marian argued that the bill would actually strengthen poor families by providing better child care for working mothers.

The veto of the bill "absolutely shattered" Marian. "We tried again the next year," she recalls, "but by then the right wing had discovered us, and the volume of hate mail scared a lot of people off."

But the experience taught her a valuable lesson: no group has less political power

than children. They can't vote or run for
office, and they can't make campaign contributions. Marian learned that the more
specific her goals, the better chance she
stood of achieving them. While children
were important to her program, they were
still just part of the bigger picture. She
now decided children were a big enough
issue in themselves. After all, they are "the
future of America." If they are allowed to
fail, how can America succeed? "That was
really the beginning of looking at children
and their unmet needs as a new way to
build a coalition for social change," Marian
says.

In 1971, the Edelmans moved to Boston
with their two young sons, Joshua and
Jonah. Peter became a vice-president at
the University of Massachusetts. Marian
headed Harvard University's Center for
Law and Education. Despite her new job,
Marian traveled to Washington once a
week to continue her work with the Washington Research Project.

Two years later, the Washington Research
Project became the Children's Defense
Fund (CDF). With the new name came a
new direction. Marian began to devote her
full energies to the cause of the nation's 50
million children.

DEAR LORD
BE GOOD TO ME
THE SEA IS SO
WIDE AND
MY BOAT IS
SO SMALL

Children's Day
A Celebration of Children
Sunday, June 13, 1982   The Washington Cath

1 pm Picnic on the Cathedral Ground

4 pm Children's Sabbath Interfaith Servic

Chapter 4

Helping the Helpless

Marian Wright Edelman sees the fight for children's rights as a war that must be fought daily. But her "fund" for their defense includes much more than money. This fund is rich in something even more precious—knowledge.

Marian visits with one of the many children who have been helped by the CDF.

A wise man once said "Knowledge is power." Marian truly believed this. Once people, especially in government, knew the facts of how children in the United States suffer, she felt they would be moved to act. If they didn't act, she saw it as CDF's job to push them to act.

Lobbying in Washington

Here is how Marian defined her job in her "60 Minutes" interview: "We spend a great deal of our time doing research and identifying the problems that affect millions of children . . . . and then we say what ought to be done about those problems.

(Opposite page)
Marian organizes a group of children for a special picnic in 1982.

And then we lobby . . . we try to enforce the laws that are already on the books."

A lobbyist is a person who tries to get legislators in Congress to introduce or support new laws that are favorable to the cause he or she represents. That special interest might be a business, a group of individuals, or an organization. There are hundreds of lobbyists in Washington, many representing strong and powerful organizations. Ironically, children, who Marian calls "our most fragile and precious resource," have had no lobbyists to speak up for them. That is, until the Children's Defense Fund.

"Everyone loves children," Marian explains. "Everybody thinks it's like motherhood and apple pie. But when [politicians] get into the budget rooms, or behind closed doors—to really decide how they're going to carve up money—children get lost in the process because they are not powerful."

The 1970s was not the best time for CDF to try to convince Congress to give more money to children's needs. After the promise of the sixties, the seventies were something of a disappointment. Too many Americans were tired of causes and seemed

Marian gives a speech at the offices of the Children's Defense Fund.

more involved in watching out for themselves than for the other person.

This mood was reflected in the domestic conservatism of the Republican administrations of presidents Richard Nixon and

Statistics from the Children's Defense Fund

- Every 35 seconds an infant is born into poverty.
- Every 2 minutes an infant is born at low birthweight (less than 5 pounds, 8 ounces).
- Every 14 minutes an infant dies in the first year of life.
- Every 31 seconds an infant is born to an unmarried mother.
- Every 55 seconds an infant is born to a mother who is not a high school graduate.
- Every 32 seconds a 15- to 19-year-old woman becomes pregnant.
- Every 64 seconds an infant is born to a teenage mother.

From *The State of America's Children 1991,* by the Children's Defense Fund.

Gerald Ford. However, CDF continued to make small gains throughout the seventies. It helped increase the federal food program to the poor and lobbied for increases in the Head Start programs.

But there was little hope for another child-care bill that would meet the needs of all areas in children's lives. With the election of Democratic President Jimmy Carter in 1976, it looked like things would improve. The Carter administration appeared to be liberal and caring, but was conservative when it came to spending money.

Rather than face defeat on a child-care bill, Marian decided to focus her efforts where they could do the most good. "We decided to concentrate on trying to expand Head Start significantly," she said in an interview. The strategy worked. Over the next four years, Congress doubled the funding for Head Start. Marian also worked to gain support for child welfare and child health improvement. Due largely to these efforts, Congress enacted a child-welfare bill in 1980.

Hard Times in a New Administration

The Edelmans moved back to Washington in 1979. Peter got a job teaching at the Georgetown University Law Center, and Marian now devoted her full efforts to lobbying for CDF.

Peter Edelman has worked on developing many social programs during his career in Washington.

She would need to give it all her energy. In 1980, Republican Ronald Reagan won the presidency, defeating Jimmy Carter. It was one of the biggest landslide victories in a presidential election. The conservative Reagan administration began to take apart the welfare system that the Democrats had built nearly 20 years before.

The modest gains made by CDF in the 1970s were quickly lost in the early 1980s. Marian compared her position to "being caught in an avalanche." According to CDF statistics, by 1987, 12.5 million children were living in poverty, about one out of every five children in the United States.

But these overwhelming odds did not discourage Marian or her staff. If new laws to protect children could not be enacted, they would fight to preserve the laws that remained on the books. The CDF continued to turn out reports. Marian used reams of statistics as her ammunition when she went to Capitol Hill to face the powerful politicians.

When President Ronald Reagan took office, his administration quickly erased many of the gains made by the CDF. By 1987, the CDF estimated that 12.5 million children were living in poverty.

Many of these statistics were alarming. Black children were twice as likely as white children to be born premature. They were twice as likely to die during the first year of life. And they were twice as likely to live in substandard housing or in an institution. They were three times as likely to be poor, be in foster care, or die of child abuse. "A black infant in Chicago is more likely to die in the first year of life than an infant in Cuba or Costa Rica," she said. It was her way of helping people understand how far behind the United States had fallen in caring for its children—black and white alike.

In addition to the flow of statistics, CDF began in 1981 to issue a yearly report called "A Children's Defense Budget." It quickly became required reading for many members of Congress.

Then in 1983, while putting together a book entitled *Black and White Children in America,* Marian made a startling discovery: 37.9 percent of all black babies were born to teenage mothers, many of whom were unmarried.

The Children's Defense Fund had found a new issue to bring before the nation. And this issue would expand its focus at a critical time in the group's development.

Chapter 5

The 101st Senator

The Children's Defense Fund's shift of focus from children to their mothers might have surprised some people. But it was a logical step for Marian Wright Edelman and her organization.

She believed the endless cycle of poverty, malnutrition, and neglect could only be broken, if unwed teen mothers stopped having children they couldn't support. Many of these mothers were barely out of childhood themselves.

Preventing Teenage Pregnancy

"Each year, 1.1 million American teen girls—one in ten—become pregnant," Marian wrote in an article in *Ebony* magazine. "Each day more than 3,000 girls get pregnant and 1,300 give birth." This adds up to half a million babies born to teenagers each year. The cost is high—to the girls, their children, and the public.

Marian in 1985.

(Opposite page)
Marian's dedication to protecting children has been the driving force in her life. She calls children "our most fragile and precious resource." *43*

It's like being grounded for eighteen years.

Having a baby when you're a teenager takes away more than your freedom, it takes away your dreams.
The Children's Defense Fund.

The CDF uses ads that are simple but effective.

According to CDF figures, the public pays $1.4 million each year to help with these births and infant care. The mothers of these children will earn about half of the life-time income of a woman who waits until the age of 20 to have her first child.

Marian concluded that the number of children born out of wedlock had reached a level that essentially guaranteed the poverty of black children for the foreseeable future. "Preventing children from having children therefore must be a high priority for every one of us."

But how to reach these teen girls and help them to help themselves? To get the message out, CDF turned to a time-honored American tradition—advertising. They put up eye-catching posters in subway stations and bus stops where youths were sure to see them. They put out press releases and donated public service announcements to radio and television.

These mass media ads pointed out the dangers of pregnancy without preaching. Marian wisely realized that preaching would only turn off the young people she needed to reach.

The posters were fresh, original, and thought provoking. In one, a teen mother was shown with her baby in her arms. The caption read: "The one on the left [the baby] will finish high school before the one on the right." Another poster showed a commercially manufactured Home Pregnancy Test. Below it were the words, "125,000 junior high students flunked this simple test last year."

But the ad campaign was just one weapon in CDF's fight against teen pregnancy. Marian established the Adolescent Pregnancy Prevention Clearinghouse. This agency offered information and technical assistance to local prevention programs across the country.

AN EXTRA SEVEN POUNDS COULD KEEP YOU OFF THE FOOTBALL TEAM.

Become a father before you're ready and you may always wonder what else you could have been.
THE CHILDREN'S DEFENSE FUND

A primary goal of the CDF is to educate teens on the subject of birth control.

Not getting pregnant was only half of CDF's message. The other half was aimed at keeping teens in school and building their self-confidence through activities in and out of the classroom. It also meant improving work-related skills, so young people could find decent jobs when they left school. For those youths who remained sexually active, it was critical that they be educated about contraceptives and other forms of birth control. CDF worked tirelessly in all these areas.

Marian, however, had no illusions of instant success: "Making a significant dent in any major social problem requires a lot of hard work and persistence over a long period of time."

Marian Wright Edelman—One View

"A soft-spoken, fast-talking woman with an engaging smile, Mrs. Edelman is the product of the civil rights movement of the 1960s. The militancy is still there, surfacing at times when she speaks of the "injustices" against her constituents or when she flashes impatience with those who say her goals, while laudable, are not always practicable in a time of tight Federal budgets. But this mother of three sons has transferred her marching and protesting energy to the halls of Congress, the offices of Federal agencies, and the courtroom."

—*The New York Times,* February 27, 1986

Lobbyist and Author

One area that Marian never neglected was congressional lobbying. Senator Edward Kennedy of Massachusetts, a supporter and admirer, has called her the "101st senator of children's issues. She has real power in Congress and uses it brilliantly."

Her husband Peter claims she has "an absolutely superb strategic and tactical sense . . . . She understands how the system works. She's as tough and determined as anyone can be, but always within the rules of the system."

Marian herself puts it in more down-to-earth terms. "There's no great magic about it. You just have to stay on people and make it easier for them to do what you want them to do than not to do it," she says. "I'm a good pest is what I am."

Her efforts were beginning to be recognized outside of the nation's capital. In 1983, the *Ladies Home Journal* named her one of the 100 most influential women in America. In 1985, she was named a MacArthur Foundation Prize Fellow. The following year, she delivered the prestigious W.E.B. DuBois Lectures at Harvard University. In 1987, these lectures were published by Harvard University Press in a

"Resist quick fix, simplistic answers, and easy gains. They often disappear just as quickly as they come."

book entitled *Families in Peril: An Agenda for Social Change.*

In the book, Marian pulled no punches: "As adults we are responsible for meeting the needs of children. It is our moral obligation. We brought about their births and their lives, and they cannot fend for themselves." Interviewed for another book, *Voices of Freedom,* she said, "This country will have to confront the issues on investing in its children and families if it is going to preserve the future."

A New Mood in America

By 1988, Marian Edelman felt more hopeful about the future than she had in years. The mood of indifference toward social problems that was so common in the eighties had finally begun to disappear. Americans were becoming concerned about the disturbing growth in the number of homeless people. The growth of widespread poverty and hunger in the richest nation on earth shocked many people. Child abuse and neglect, subjects often hidden in the past, were now making headlines in newspapers and magazines.

Presidential contenders George Bush and Michael Dukakis both addressed the growing need for day care for children of

Marian speaks at a CDF meeting in 1985.

mothers forced to enter the workplace. As a reflection of this new concern, the year 1988 was declared "the year of the child" by William Harris, president of Kidspac, a political-action group.

Marian decided the time was right to do something she had wanted to do for a long time—put together another comprehensive child-care bill and propose it to Congress. Unlike her previous attempt 17 years before, Marian felt this time she could succeed.

Chapter 6

Making a Difference

Marian worked on her new bill for close to a year. She and her staff discussed the details with 170 different individuals and organizations. She asked what they thought should be included to meet the most urgent needs of America's children. She called the bill "ABC," which stood for "Act for Better Child Care."

Marian, around 1987.

A Landmark Bill

When finished, ABC was impressive. It called for $2.5 billion to be spent in just the first year it was enacted. The money would mostly go to helping families with low and moderate income. It would help them pay for child care. The bill was also designed to enforce the highest standards of quality, health, and safety for child care for all children.

While Marian was lobbying to get her bill passed by Congress, another child-care bill

(Opposite page)
Marian addresses a crowd at a Children's Defense Fund rally in Washington, D.C., 1990.

CDF supporters gather in front of the Capitol in 1990.

was making the rounds. It was introduced by Utah's conservative senator Orrin Hatch. Marian didn't feel the Hatch bill called for enough money. It also allowed states to control how the funds would be spent, which Marian didn't like. She knew from her experience years before in Mississippi that local lawmakers didn't always act in the best interests of their people.

But Marian found two lawmakers who believed strongly in her ABC bill. They were representatives Tom Downey of New York and George Miller of California. These two men helped to get ABC passed in the House of Representatives, where it went in August 1988.

The bill received little support from either presidential candidate that election year. George Bush promoted his own "children's tax credit" for working parents, Michael Dukakis showed little enthusiasm for ABC in his campaign. This was a bitter disappointment to Marian, who expected better from the Democratic candidate.

In the end, despite support from 38 senators and 172 representatives, the bill was stalled on the floor of Congress. It was pulled out before a final vote. Marian was angry.

"Politicians do not have a lot of courage," she later said. "Both parties used the bill as a political plaything."

In June 1989, the Senate proposed a new bill authorizing $1.2 billion in grants for child care and tax credits to working parents. This was only half of what the ABC bill had asked for, but was still a lot of money.

Both Downey and Miller, in an apparent change of heart, were skeptical. They felt that the Senate would actually spend only a small portion of the authorized money when the time came. But they wanted to make sure the available money would be safe from budget cuts and changes.

"Don't be afraid of taking risks or of being criticized. It's the way you learn to do things right."

Downey and Miller, along with other liberal legislators, now viewed ABC as the kind of broad-sweeping legislation popular in the 1960s. Such a bill, they thought, had little chance of success in the nineties, where money would not be spent so freely.

Creating good child care laws is one of Marian's top concerns.

Marian Wright Edelman—Another View

"When Marian Wright Edelman comes to visit, it's as though a genial storm has blown in. She is electric in promotion of her cause, America's children. She throws out facts like hailstorms. Her voice, like the wind, is alternately sharp and playful. Her critique of America's perverse priorities is thunderous. She is a powerhouse of commitment and energy, and God knows she needs to be, for America's insensitivity to the fate of its children is like a stone wall that only powerful persistence can break through."

—*The Charlotte Observer,* February 16, 1990

Out of her frustration in November 1989, Marian released an angry letter addressed to representatives Downey and Miller. She accused them of acting "to sabotage ground-breaking child-care legislation." This conflict over tactics, fueled by the letter from Marian, caused a split in the child-care forces. Congress ended up backing the new proposal and totally disregarding ABC as unworkable.

While the final grant of $600 million fell far short of what Marian believed was needed, it was three times what Miller and Downey had asked for. In a sense, Marian both won and lost the battle. She helped pave the way for a new child care bill, but she also may have lost influential friends for future Congressional fights. But that possibility does not worry her: "The day I wonder about my popularity is the day we lose our effectiveness."

Powerful Friends Help the Cause

As luck would have it, Marian's popularity actually soared in 1992. With the election of her longtime friend and admirer Bill Clinton as president of the United States, Marian's power and influence increased significantly. Not only was the new president a strong supporter of Marian and her work, the First Lady—Hillary Rodham Clinton—was the former chairperson of the CDF. Mrs. Clinton, like her husband, had only the greatest admiration for Marian. In fact, Hillary had been previously quoted as saying Marian Wright Edelman was her "idol." When the Clintons moved into the White House in January 1993, a new era dawned for Marian and her cause.

Throughout 1992 and 1993, America really got to know Marian Wright Edelman. During the president's many special advisory meetings on health-care reform and social welfare policy, Hillary was often seen sitting on one side of the president while

Marian was on the other. Debates about public health care and social reform once again became pressing topics all across the United States. And Marian frequently joined the debate on television and radio. In addition, she also published a book entitled *The Measure of Our Success*, which discussed the problems of children and the poor in America and proposed solutions. Her book remained on the bestseller list for many months. It seemed that the world was finally ready to listen to Marian Wright Edelman's message.

"Never think life is not worth living or that you cannot make a difference. Never give up."

Continuing the Fight

Today, at age 56, Marian Wright Edelman is a vibrant, optimistic woman who works hard, but never at the expense of her family. In this sense, she practices what she preaches. She has instilled high standards for excellence in her three sons. Her eldest son, Joshua, recently graduated from Harvard; Jonah studied at Yale; and Ezra, the youngest, is a graduate of Sidwell Friends School in Washington.

Marian is an enthusiastic reader, both on and off the job. Just keeping up with her own publications must take up a good share of her reading time. The Children's Defense Fund now has a staff of 90. They

Though her schedule is hectic, Marian still takes time out to be with the many who benefit from the CDF.

turn out 2,000 pages of reports each year. Their dramatic statistics and up-to-date figures continue to have an impact on the people in power all across the country who read them.

What does the future hold for CDF and Marian Wright Edelman? It is hard to say.

Her influence—though always powerful–
depends on the administration in the
White House. Certainly, with Bill Clinton
in the Oval Office, Marian remains one of
the most powerful voices in Washington.
And she has many supporters as well. One
of the most vocal, surprisingly, is Orrin
Hatch, who risked offending his own conservative supporters to back the child care
issue. It was Senator Hatch who helped
put together the Senate child-care bill.

"I think she is the single most effective
spokesman for child care in America
today," Hatch has said. "She is a strong,
formidable, forceful advocate, and some-
times that stings us . . . and I'm one of the
ones who's been stung by Marian, because
we don't always agree. But I've got to say
that she's very good, very effective, and she
knows what she's talking about."

Meanwhile, the work of CDF goes on.
The organization has recently started an
immunization campaign for city children
under age five. Many of these children
have never been protected against danger-
ous childhood diseases. Another concern
is Latino youths, who Marian feels need
more attention in school. Only then can
these Latinos get better jobs and break out
of the cycle of poverty. The organization is

**Marian in New Haven,
Connecticut in May, 1990.**

also working on the second phase of its campaign against teen pregnancy.

"The first phase was to point out that it's a big national problem," explains Marian. "The second phase has to do with results: setting and achieving goals . . . . It's our view that the best way to prevent teenage pregnancies is to give young people a sense of hope—a sense that they have a future. To do that, we want to strengthen basic skills, youth services, job opportunities, and recreation."

In the 26 years since Marian confronted that angry group of black youths in Mississippi, much has changed. Yet, in many ways, nothing has changed. Some conditions have improved, but Marian feels the sense of hopelessness and despair she felt in the sixties is more widespread today than ever before.

"There never was a time when I was growing up that I didn't think I could change the world," Marian has said. "I don't think young people today—enough of them—feel they can change the world."

For Marian Wright Edelman the fight continues, day by day, moment to moment. If there is fear, hunger, and hurt felt by even one child in America, this dedicated and compassionate woman will not rest.

Glossary

Explaining New Words

day care A place outside the home where working parents can leave their pre-school children during working hours.

demonstration A gathering of people to protest against a law or other public or government policy that they oppose.

discrimination The treatment of a group of people differently from other people because of their race, religion, age, ethnic background, or sex.

legislator An elected member of Congress who works to make laws.

lobbyist A person who tries to get lawmakers to support laws favorable to the special interest group he or she represents.

segregation A policy of keeping black Americans separated from whites, politically, socially, and economically. It was prevalent in many parts of the United States until the 1960s.

For Further Reading

Edelman, Marian. *Families in Peril: An Agenda for Social Change.* Cambridge: Harvard University Press, 1987.

— "How to Prevent Teenage Pregnancy." *Ebony,* July, 1987.

— *Portrait of Inequality: Black and White Children in America.* Washington, D.C.: Children's Defense Fund, 1980.

— "Save the Children." *Ebony,* August, 1986.

— "Selling the Shadow for the Substance." Spelman College Commencement address, May, 1988. Children's Defense Fund, 1988.

Shapiro, Joseph P. "The Unraveling Kids' Crusade." *U.S. News and World Report,* March 26, 1990.

Tompkins, Calvin. "A Sense of Urgency." *New Yorker,* March 27, 1987.

Index

Photo credits:
Cover, pages 10, 58: © Jonathan Levine; pps. 4, 22, 31, 37, 39, 43, 51: AP/Wide World Photos; pps.
5, 7, 8, 12, 34, 44–45: Children's Defense Fund; p. 13: © Marc Riboud/Magnum Photos, Inc.; pps. 15,
25: Office of Public Information, Yale University; p. 16: © Danny Lyon/Magnum Photos, Inc.; p. 17:
Stanford University News and Publication Service; p. 19: © Marion Post/FSA, Library of Congress;
pps. 20, 32: © Bruce Davidson/Magnum Photos, Inc.; p. 23: UPI/Bettmann; p. 24: © Elliott Erwitt/
Magnum Photos, Inc.; p. 27: © Cornell Capa/Magnum Photos, Inc.; pps. 35, 42, 54: © Rick Rein-
hard/Children's Defense Fund; p. 40: Reuters/Bettmann; p. 49 © Richard Greenhouse/Children's
Defense Fund; pps. 50, 52: © Peggy Harrison/Children's Defense Fund; p. 59: © Richard Glassman.

Photo Research by Inge King.